# REASONS WHY

# WHY

# I ❤ YOU

FROM: _____

TO: _____

# Author's Note

No matter how you express your love to your partner, one of the best ways is to let him/her know by directly letting your partner how you feel or think about it.

With this book, I hope you will find this book a perfect keepsake, a love token, which will remind you of a unique relationship you and your partner built together.

**1**

I LOVE YOU BECAUSE YOU NEVER SAY NO
WHEN I

_____

# 2

## The most attractive thing when I first met you

_____

**3**

# When I have hard times, You always

_____

**4**

I feel

_____

WHEN YOU'RE BY MY SIDE

# 5

## WHEN I LOOK INTO YOUR EYES, I FEEL LIKE

_____

**6**

I LOVE SPENDING TIMES DOING

_____

WITH YOU.

# 7

## I FEEL SAFE, WHEN YOU

_____

**8**

I HAVE ALWAYS WANTED TO

_____

WITH YOU.

# 9

# Your simple thing that is very special to me

_____

# 10

## THE WAY YOU MAKE ME LOVE YOU MORE

_____

# 11

## When I think of you, I always want to

_____

# 12

Ha-ha-ha ...

# The Secret thing, Others don't know But you

---

# 13

When I'm nervous, You always

_____

# 14

I REALLY LOVE WHEN YOU

FLIRT ME BY

_____

# 15

# THE BEST GIFT I'VE EVER
# RECEIVED FROM YOU

# 16

You Look Like My Lovely pup

That Is

_____

# 17

## My Relationship Goal with

## You is

_____

# 18

## As We Grow up Together,
## You Still

_____

**19**

_____

IS MY FAVORITE MOMENT
WITH YOU.

# 20

## The Warmness Of your Hug
## Makes Me Feel Like

_____

# 21

## I Love When You Called me

_____

# 22

# I'm Really In The Mood
# When You

_____

**23** DRAW SOMETHING

YOU'RE MY

_____

IN MY REAL LIFE.

# 24

## You Always Know When I'm Going To

_____

**25**

*good*
*morning*

I Love When We

_____

In The Morning.

# 26

## Your Kiss Tastes Like

_____

**27**

Even I'm mad at You, You Still

_____

# 28

# I Love How We Help Each Other By

_____

# 29

I Love When You See This
World as If

_____

**30**

# YOU CAN DO iT

## You Let Me

_____

## Even I'm Terrible With It

**31**

Is The Little Things that Really Means A Lot To Me

# 32

I'm Always Filled With Joy
When You.

_____

**33**

I Really Love The Way You

_____

# 34

I Believe When You Grow Old
You Would Be Like

**35**

I Love The Way You

_____

My Family.

# 36

## Believe
### IN
### yourself

YOU ALWAYS DO

---

WHICH IS IMPOSSIBLE FOR ME

# 37

I Always That Someone has My
Back, Because You Have Become My
Bigeest Source Of

---

# 38

When I'm With You, Is The Time When I'm Totally

_____

**39**

BAD TIMES ALWAYS FEEL

_____

WHEN YOU _____

**40**

# yes

YOU NEVER SAY NO WHEN I

_____

# 41

## THE MOST MEMORABLE GIFT, I'VE RECIEVED

**42**

You Have The Greatest Taste In

_____

**43**

I'M KIND OF OBSESSED WITH YOUR

_____

**44**

BEING_____

IS YOUR SUPERPOWER.

# 45

## WHEN YOU INTRODUCED ME TO

_____

## IT'S CHANGED MY LIFE.

**46**

THAT'S_____ PART OF YOURS

I WANT TO KNOW IT MORE!

**47**

I'll Always support Your

_____

You Know, You Always Have My Back.

# 48

## THE MORE WE SPEND TIME TOGETHER , THE MORE SURE I AM

**49**

THE BEST COMPLIMENT, I EVER
RECEIVED FROM YOU IS

_____

**50**

My Future Goal I Always Dream To Do With You Is

_____

And I Wish That We'll Be Always

_____

Printed in Great Britain
by Amazon